THE IMAGINATION BEING

Michael A. Susko

AllrOneofUs Publishing
Baltimore, Md & Huntsville, Al

While every precaution has been taken in the preparation of this book, the publisher assumes no responsibility for errors or omissions, or for damages resulting from the use of the information contained herein.

THE IMAGINATION BEING

First edition. October 10, 2021.

ISBN: 979-8215910313

Written by Michael A. Susko.

Also by Michael A. Susko

A Couple Through Time
Down Below and the Archon's Castle
Up Above and the Runaway
Across the Gulf and Journey Into Un-Time
On the Bay and a Child Found
In the Wild and Do One Wild Thing
On the Mountain and Two Are Missing
To the Beginning and Journey Through Here

Archetypal Worlds
Alwon in Another World: An Archetypal Voyage
Line On the Wall
The Alien's Gift
The Gold People
Spider Woman and the Timeroc
Quill Ears & the Other Earth
Darkwood and Dual with the Shadow Side
Giant Under the Mountain

Early Humanity

The Firekeeper
Child of the Elements

Haikus and Photos
Flowers and Haikus
Haikus and Photos: Guatemalan Highlands
Haikus and Photos: Water Birds and Reflections
Haikus and Photos: Seasons of New River
Haikus and Photos: Yosemite Wilderness
Haikus and Photos: California Coast
Haikus and Photos: Canadian Rockies
Haikus and Photos: Hawaii's Exotic Landscapes
Haikus and Photos: Vienna, People with Buildings and Art
Haikus and Photos: Slovakian Castles and Hamlets
Haikus and Photos: Berlin, Light and Dark
Haikus and Photos: New Orleans, City of Immigrants
Haikus and Photos: Antietam Wind and Spirits
Haikus & Photos: Plant Abstractions
Haikus and Photos: Appalachian Beauty
Haikus and Photos: Urban Farm in Sandtown
Haikus and Photos: New York Heights and Ground

Little Lion
The Lion and the Chameleon
The Elephant and the Chameleons

Nature Haikus & Photos
Haikus and Photos: Butterflies and Flowers

Haikus and Photos: A Cardinal's Life
Haikus and Photos: Two Racoons at Play
Haikus and Photos: Hawaiian Green Sea Turtle
Haikus and Photos: Irises in the Rain
Haikus and Photos: The Mystic Iris
Haikus and Photos: Tulip Opening

Second Mystery Stone from the Shenandoah
Haikus & Photos: 2nd Shenandoan Mystery Stone
Haikus and Photos: 2nd Mystery Stone 3-D Forms

Shenandoan Stone Explorations
Mystery Stone from the Shenandoah
Philosopher Stone from the Lower Shenandoah
Beyond the Portal: From Within the Mystery Stone
The Mystery of Essence
Gifts from the Indigenous: Six Awarenesses & Six Doings

Shenandoan Stone: Haikus & Photos
Haikus and Photos: Cosmogram from the Shenandoah
Haikus and Photos: Woodland Mystery Stone and World Archetypes
Haikus and Photos: Skeletal Human and Mississippian Art
Haikus and Photos: Mystery Stone's Animal Forms
Haikus and Photos: Plant Forms and Mystery Stone

Stone Formation at Penn Bluff

Haikus and Photos: Presence at Penn Bluff
Haikus & Photos: Mystery Form at Penn Bluff
Haikus and Photos: Essences at Penn Bluff
Haikus and Photos: World Archetypes at Penn Bluff

The Dreaming Series
Sleek Back
Streak and Cave Bear Dreaming
Moby and Marsupial Mole Dreaming

The Dream World Trilogy
Delphi, the Time Thief, and the Dream World
Detinna and the Cave God
The Resistance & the Empire

Transformational Stories
Caseness and Narrative: Contrasting Approaches to People
Psychiatrically Labelled
Transformative Experiences, Psychiatric Research, and Informed
Consent
Transformational Stories: Voices for True Healing in Mental Health

Writings from Street People
Street Images
Street Images II

Table of Contents

For those who journey with their imagination to find answers for this world.

CHAPTER I
THE START

I am alone. The surrounding land I don't recognize. There are no friends present. I am not sure even what type of being I am. I am in a realm that society has been diminishing and redirecting toward its own materialist, militaristic, and even racist ends. I begin by envisioning a new being—consistent with what Mozi, the ancient Chinese philosopher, calls the *Universal.* It's not based on discriminating or the assertion that you are better or superior to others, whoever they may be, and by whatever criteria.

So the being I am unearthing is an *Imagination Being,* like a childhood imaginary friend, but holding more substance than that.

I make an empty space for it to come into being, to aid me and for me to be filled. Let it take shape.

It starts as a lump of light, soft and moldable. A gentle light bending and forming easily in my mind's hands. Leaving a soft after glow on my palms, I gently press on the doughy light. It takes the form of a person. How can it be more comfortable than that? I need not try to find something better. Nor do I need to add wings to make it a supernatural being. Does it have a sex? Or is it unsexed, or both sexes? I run into the problem of whether to refer to the being as he, she, or an it.

It is hard to start a new language, and I could go back to the old-fashioned Thou, reserved for the divine. This being, while not imagined as divinity itself, goes in that direction, for it is of a pure and holy essence, a higher self/soul if you will, if I might be allowed to speak plainly.

I do not mean that this being will be easy to understand, that it will not have unfathomability, or that I have fully determined what it is. It will be gradually be uncovered and tied into an archetype or some principality of the universe. I hope that it will have wisdom and secrets to divulge for those willing to encounter, ask, and access this being.

I sense it is there. It occurs to me to ask a question.

CHAPTER II
QUESTION

I ask, feeling that the question will help the Being take further shape. "Why am I here? Why are you here? Why is anything here?"

Forgive me, but that is three questions, but they seem very related. Perhaps I could have asked the *how* I got here, and that might lead to the *why*. Perhaps, though, there is no why and that I need to consider as well. Or, if there is a why, maybe the answer is co-created between you and me, and not just dictated from above. Whatever the answers may be, you and I are here, and there can be no doubt about that.

My questions remain and the Being pulsates as if to register them.

It answers, "All of what you think has its truth. The why will be discovered if you seek but deeper."

"Where do you find the answers then?"

"Are they not within you? Not in travels that eventually must return, nor in electronic screens which detain you with a cascade of messages."

"So it's within, I repeat. How do I go there?" Already, questions lead to questions, and perhaps I am further from what I first asked. But is attempting to find answers a path itself and not simply words I gather? Already, my why has turned into a how.

"The answers are already surfacing from within," the Being responds. "Some are just below, while others are much deeper and one must plummet to find them. The deep questions and their full answers are the path of a lifetime."

"Is there a way I should use--a meditation or yoga pose, where I close my eyes and delve into my inner self? Do I take a walk with you, where perhaps the landscape will form and match my inner journey?"

"Within or without," says the Being. "They reflect each other. But the journey within provides the direction you seek. The deeper you go, the truer you must be. I warn you, there are guardians at the gate, and the deeper path is one people usually steer away from or avoid."

"Help me then," I ask. "I am weak on the journey. I know this much."

"You may start anew," the Being allowed. "Close your eyes and see what comes to you. There is no amount of time for how long or how short it takes to come to you. It may come in a moment; it may take hours. When it comes, you will know and note it. Start now."

I willingly obeyed.

I closed my eyes, and it wasn't long, as I noted the background din, that I heard a simple yet deep message.

"I love you. I am the Fountain."

The question quickly arose. Who declares its love? Was it the Being, or something beyond the Being? The word was near to the surface.

There is the teaching that "God is love." Yet the word was more precise than that. That love is a fountain, an act of flowing. It is not a noun, complete and closed on itself, but a verb.

"Good," said the Being. "Try again, close your eyes, and see what more comes."

The next message followed soon, with just some disrupting thoughts. "Serve others, even if it hurts. The hurt may be a sign that it is necessary."

"Why, I ask, is it so hard to do something that is good for us to do, and even avoid it? It is something that will make us feel much better afterwards. It is a mystery to me."

The Light Being glimmered. "It takes asking to search out this answer. "

"Yes, I know the saying, 'Ask and you shall receive.'"

"To ask is much of the battle. As for the answer, it will be tested for self-will intrudes with its intoxication. *It wants what it wants.* It likes this power, one that leaves a self-satisfying glow. To break through the dark barrier of selflessness is a death. Even though resurrection is promised, no one wants to die. Even Jesus asked that this suffering pass."

The mention of Jesus made me wonder about his relation to the Light Being.

"Living the selfless way involves many small deaths," the Light Being went on. "It involves dropping your normal flow. Sometimes it is amid your day to day work. However it happens, the net effect of this dying is to give life."

"To know is not to do," I said. "How can I *do* what I know is best and yet find myself *not doing* it?"

"Grace, a wellspring, enables you, if only the bit that is needed."

"I think I must close my eyes again," I responded. "More is needed to unlock this heart of mine, which is open and guarded at the same time."

"It is good to cast far and near, and go back to the center."

I try, but there is no message––only a welter of confusion and many scattered ideas at once.

"Go past that, or under it," said the guide.

CHAPTER III
PEACE

I try again and a dozen more things come to mind that don't add to a coherent image or message. Finally, one word does: *Peace*. Whatever our limits, whatever our failings, with all the not-yet about us, we can return to Peace, which is close to the center.

"I have found something close to the center: a Peace within ourselves and a Peace found with others. Hopefully, we carry our lives forward with this Peace, and then we will rest in Peace when our journey is done."

While I uttered these thoughts, the Light Being's aureole became fringed with blue, which I believed signaled Peace.

"It is something that you can ask for," said the Being. "For all your life you have struggles, strivings and failings—winnings as well, which are perhaps taken for granted."

"It feels good to remember the winnings," I said. "I think I felt a few moments of it."

"Yes, draw upon Peace, become Peace. There is so much that wars and would war in the world."

"Yet I know there is a spiritual war to be fought."

"For now, meditate upon peace. Try to become Peace, to be near to peace."

"There is no shortage of pain at any stage in our journey," I reflected after a long moment. "There are always new challenges, and the new ones are not easier than the old."

"It is a good sign to have challenges. They are gifts too," said the Light Being.

"There is more joy, too. I have been blessed."

"But it seems, from the other side, that I am somewhat friendless, with little love. Then too, how do I wrestle with a sexual energy that seeks its outlet?"

"You have love, a son and a wife, and brothers, and church friends—more for you to but follow up upon. As for sexuality, it is a gift, yet one that needs to be directed and channeled toward a good end."

"My projects fall short. There needs to be something more."

"There is more. There is real presence, real prayer. You can call upon me. I am a mystical friend."

"Is there a name you go by?"

"For now, it is better that I remain nameless and let my name
be discovered by you."

"Names ... In scripture Solomon built a house for the name of the High One."

"Yes, there is honor on those who house the name. But now close your eyes and await something more."

I do, and messages come in short phrases:

Double Peace
Then an image:
A cross with a heart
A knotted heart with a cross reaching out...
Light—
Wood becoming light
There's pain and new life...

Another day, I still need to be fed with words. I need to close my eyes again. The Being is patient and gentle, waiting.

I love you
I am with you

I am many things
With you,
In your failings, too
Know that
Keep steady
Testing is a sign that big things await
Stay the course...

"Yes, it's reassuring. But why are things so hard at the end of the day?"

"Of course, you know it is like death. We let go...."

"I need to let go so I can have time to work and study, to make discoveries that are like you. So many words. Don't I need to be with someone?"

"That is available. You need to wrestle alone some first."

"Take me somewhere, even if it is in an imaginary realm. I need to travel. Fortunately, it is free to move the soul. It takes someone with time, though."

"Time has been granted to you. Close our eyes and come with me."

"I am dancing, twirling among lawns and greenery."

"We dance and draw people into the dance," says the Light Being.

"You have let me be free. But the world is often so different. Why do we want to control others?" I asked.

"Because perhaps everyone knows that wisdom is not contained in any one person. The other never fails to see the wisdom you need and so tries to give it."

"What wisdom would you give me this morning?"

"Always, like Solomon, seek wisdom, ask for it, and the Universe, boundless as it is, will grant it."

I am at the gateway of this land, unable to fully enter. So I close my eyes again to receive a new message. But I know the new word before I do so. It is giving and what follows from acts of giving. It makes you feel right with the universe. Still, I will meditate and see what more is provided.

Giving is the reason for being
And receiving as well
We receive life's breath
Then give our life to others

The Light Being was happy, it seemed, for it glowed brighter. Its face took form, revealing a beauty whose intensity was such that it could only be viewed for a few moments before it receded into a diffuse glow that was its general presence.

"You touch upon a mystery," said the Being.

"Why, I ask, does giving make one feel so good afterwards?"

"If we are all connected, and when you touch another being in a good way, it touches you back. It also feels good because other beings are thanking you on an invisible plane."

"I had not thought to wonder why. Some would say it strokes your own ego to know you've done something good."

"The soul can thank the soul. There is much that is *and* rather than an *or*. Many contradictory things, when fully understood, may be joined by *and*.

"Let me thank you now, if I haven't, for encouraging my meditation, for finding words that refresh my being and encourage the touching you describe."

"You are welcome into the deeper ways. But there is more; your journey has just begun."

CHAPTER IV
MESSAGES

It is time to meditate again and see what the universe provides. If the kingdom of heaven is within, and its riches are by definition inexhaustible, then I have no fear or anxiety that I will find nothing.

It takes but a moment for a message to be received:

Face Things: Face the Sin and the Good. Do not turn and run.

"It makes sense," I say. "Brief, but enough wisdom to hold the day. For to face things, even though it may not be resolved, is purgative and offers an opening for hope. Something unfaced is more likely to fester, to come back and be controlling in indirect ways. You must honestly face honestly your faults and your good––to see both clearly, for both are of equal importance."

"You are gaining wisdom," said the Being.

"It is like your thoughts ... like your mind and mine are merging more."

"All things are joined from the inside. There's a synchronicity in the heart of things. In the spirit domain, it is called the communion of saints. *Who* is speaking dissolves, in part, into all who are speaking, or could have spoken."

"It seems my next step is to face the good and the bad within myself. I suppose it is best to see the bad first. For one must remove the tarnish and encrustation that keeps one from seeing the good in oneself."

"A good choice," said the Being of Light. "Fear not."

I envision demons, various types, and one with a burnished, rugged face. Immediately, I want to know why it takes pleasure in another's diminishment, in making someone less than they are.

"My progress is to compare the face of someone from what they could be to what they have fallen to," says the demon.

"Why do you care to do that?" I ask, not having the faintest clue.

The demon asks back, "Why do you think people choose the wrong? Is there not a reason why?"

I fear going too deep into an exchange with this master of lies, who will twist things and bring in hidden distortions.

I take a sword and attack the demons. From where the sword came, whether by my thought or gift of the imaginary being, is not clear. I remembered an angel with a sword casting humanity from paradise and the archangel expelling the false angel of light from paradise....

I cut these demons in half. It's something I'll need to do every day....

The demons are gone for now and I wonder, *What is my sin?*

I focus on one: acquiring and indulging in wisdom without sharing it. I think of ways of spreading the light and what hinders me from taking them. *Why do I not share?*

There is always risk of rejection, naysaying, and being hurt by others out of envy. It is safer to hide oneself under a bushel, or so it seems.

But in the end, there is joy in giving and making things manifest.

"You can do it more readily than you think," said the Being. "You know the steps necessary in this day and age."

The simple process begins again, to close my eyes and see what emerges from within, for through this archetype, I tap into a universal reality.

This time I receive but a word: *Enjoy.* It asks if you are having fun, are engaged, and if time passes with delight and ease. Am I constrained by a job that we only endure? Has the time come to reevaluate, to quit and do something new?

"To enjoy is not to just seek pleasure. It is a state of being, to be *en -joy*. So I go about making assorted discoveries I do not share."

"The completion of joy is with others, to love others as yourself," the Being teaches. "It reverberates back and forth."

"We are we so fallen? We do things so imperfectly. Even a simple good thing is hard to do. The walls around us are so thick and tall."

"Yet, grace is given, and it's just enough or a little more to take the next step along our journey."

"In the end, I pray for grace and to be in a place where I can receive it. We are like a king on a podium in the temple courtyard, kneeling with outstretched arms before the people and praying for the presence of God. Even if it not all the people are present, there is the communion of Saints.... And even if we are not kings. We are sons and daughters of God, and thus more than kings."

"And if we are children of God, we enjoy being such and being nearer to God."

I close my eyes again and three words come to mind: *On the Verge.* I am on the verge of making change, of carving out a new path. What are ten things that I am on the verge of—keeping it general and not a practical to-do list?

1.) On the verge of change: a transition phase, feeling unsettled, being open to the something different.

2,) On the verge of reaching out, of putting forward more work, of being out there.

3.) On the verge of activating all avenues of artistic expression—for which more time now allows.

4.) On the verge of being willing to confront, to face and tell others the truth.

5.) On the verge of doing the small things that need to be done.

6.) On the verge of incorporating enjoyable things daily that are healthy and in line with my true work.

7.) On the verge of cutting out the last remnants of bad habits that hold me back.

8.) On the verge of spending more real time with others.

9.) On the verge of loving simply.

10.) On the verge of being there for the moment....

"Those are some good on-the-verge statements," said the Light Being. "It's good to have more than a 'to do' list, but a 'to be' list. That is more how your being flows in relation to others."

"Merge with me for a moment," I say. "Let me close my eyes so that I may draw upon your strength. A subtle love and gentle ... It is enough."

Be loving even as you go about doing things imperfectly. Another message that comes to me with closed eyes. For as we try to do good, we will be imperfect, so at least try to be loving as we do them. If go about humbly *doing,* it is bound to contain the imperfection.

"You still wrestle," said the Light Being. "The good is constantly calling us to draw closer in mind and deed. Your acts can come closer to perfection, as much as can be attained at that moment."

"I do not want to fight myself, to freeze myself. I fear too that I am afraid to put myself out there."

"And become a martyr? Would that you have that much influence! Yet it is time to put more of the wisdom you work for forward. A blog of daily thoughts hot off the mind invites a response. Things grow cold after a while and can only be reworked so much. Often, others need a word back, so they can take the next step deeper. Often enemies serve that purpose...."

"If I am in the arms of the Light Being, what do I have to fear? Everything happens within that radiance. The bad pales compared to that light, though at first it has an urgency that seems to black it out."

"If you walk bathed in such, all else is more doable, and you have found a secret. It makes possible much of the courage, much of what seems incredible. If light is bathing you, the pain of an event cannot penetrate as deeply or in the same way. Stay bathed in the light."

I close my eyes again and, like the desert fathers of old, I ask to be given a word that I may live. Each day we need a word....

Do what is necessary. Necessity is our greatest weapon. It is not all we must do, but yet we need to face the necessary of each day, and the limits of what we can do.

It is necessary to have food; it is necessary to have prayer. *How slight my prayer*, I think wistfully. *If only I would pray more.* How the empty spaces are now filled by technology, how we have become a prayerless people.... Empty moments where we could become aware of the concerns of the deeper soul are distracted by beeps and messages.

"What of the deep messages we miss?" I ask.

"Precisely," replies the Light Being. "So much intrudes, so much of the day can stand in the way."

"Why does it take a crisis to return one to the heart of things?"

"Yes, they are often a hidden blessing of life, breaking through at key times. Else, what good would you have done?"

"Why is it so hard to connect to life and love, to the center of things? It's available. Yet we go anywhere but.... We don't weather darkness, giving up of self to return to *base*, even if it be 20 seconds!"

"That is the clue. Your source knows that the day demands you. It can expand a moment into a small eternity. See how that works, even for a minute."

"Even to record the distractions in my flurry of consciousness––the female form, my word count, expectation from others..."

"A simple start, yet enough."

"So I fall, and yet I know I am loved. At times, I lose the battle of the night, which takes away the morning and its early hours of discovery."

"*You are loved.* To that return always. If you fall, you fall. Who does not? It is when you do not care to get up anymore. When you give up aspiring...."

"I am reminded of Bonaventure's seven stages of ascent. It seems I wallow in the forecourt before the first stage."

"To desire the ascent, and the journey deeper within, is to come closer to the Source. You have been given the time to seek the spiritual, to go through a redirection of your life."

"The spirit world is ever so generous, but time is limited. I am older and have limited time to do what is necessary."

"You will be given time. Respond to the promptings to finish what must be finished."

So I close my eyes again and listen to the message.

"We love you, for we are many. We are your friends.... Try to give; ask to give. That is all. Always in the waters of giving."

"I know I must share my work. I ask for the strength, wisdom, and place to do it. We are in a time in history when you can post your thoughts to the world."

"Go forward. You will find the place to do so."

"Help me find it! Grant me the grace."

"Let us bless you."

"I will be still."

"I am still and open to the grace. It makes me stronger and more upright than I really am. God is still working, a patient architect."

The message, not long in coming, I don't even close my eyes. *Peace again*, for only out of peace can spiritual warfare be sustained. Peace is also for the minor squabbles, so that the heart can be calmed, so that bigger struggles can go sustained.

It is time to act, to do something, to break out of the shell of words. "Where do we go? What do we do?"

"Come with me then, " said the Light Being.

CHAPTER V

IMAGES

"Are you sure you want to go?" asked the Light Being. "It is a wild ride. It is not predictable. It will bring images."

"Where else can I go? Who else can I trust? You have been true thus far."

"Good," said the Being. "Just do your part. Close your eyes and come to the new place."

I come to the place, hung with vegetation in three dimensions without a land beneath it. It is permeated by mind, by human feeling, impulses, and complexities of the human heart. It can be anyone, but it is only one person.

It is the space of my spouse. Islands of thoughts, not connected linearly, pulsing with different intensity. But on a trigger, ready for action.

It's a different type of mind, one not guided and ordered by set consistent internal principles, but dynamically shifting, with interacting hubs activated with different intensities. Emotionally charged. A type of logic is there and can correct or alter, but its threads are weaker and cannot always override the actionable charge.

I peer for a moment into another mind, from which I have just experienced from the outside, often without understanding and discomfort even. This visual image of another mind will enable me to navigate the shoals that I repeatedly hit and become adrift upon.

"Let me offer you images," said the Light Being, since you bounce against nothingness. "A heart beating. A heart aglow with red and yellow light beaming. A heart that is in the universe, beating out spiritual waves. Feel it; close your eyes and feel it."

"The heart is there. Whose heart? The universe, God's, mine, and all of our hearts. There is no competition between the hearts, only invitation. The seraphic seal of St. Francis ... I feel hurt, my lacking at the unfulfilled aspiration. Isn't that hurt a type of beginning?"

"How can I keep from the body the need for physicality that comes upon me at night? Are modern-day persons right, that there is no denying the body, that theological words cannot substitute?"

"You already sense the answer. Immerse gently in the light of the Presence and be transformed. Let the energy of the body diffuse into a gift for all. With bodily grace, all good is possible."

"Has not time become limited? I'm becoming lengthy in my years, long in the tooth.... Am I not already mourning my lost promise?"

"The time of realization is often later than we think it should be for us. But we can only start from where we are. There is much treasure stored, as you have been working toward the path all these years, even if not fully realized."

"Close your eyes and again follow, for this is a nurturing that can build and release to action."

"What is action? There is a mystery to it, is there not? Isn't it all we do, an action, even prayer?"

"Action is readily seen as directed to others. We act for others."

"It is time for a message? Is it time to close my eyes? *Soothing, gentle, peace.*"

"Is there an image too? Yes, a hand with light emanating, a hand alone in space, and one I know can touch softly. Whose hand it? Is it not someone unknowable, something un-named?"

"Be held in that light and discover. Be held, as you are held, and hold others."

"I need to put myself in harm's way, where others need service."

"That will come again, but today is sufficient for itself."

"All I can do is offer the day and be present to what happens. I know that even my demeanor is a gift, due more to grace that is given that to anything I have done or deserve."

Again, I do not know if there is anything more, but I need to but close my eyes and see what is present.

"The image/thought comes of the sexual zone/area/organs being filled/emitting light, diffusing to the body."

"Yes, the spirit goes to all areas, and do not leave out that which generates the new life of your kind."

"A reflection I may offer. The legs are for movement and above them is the sacrum, the center of gravity. And so much of movement is about finding/maintaining mates."

"Yes, there are literal mates and soul mates as well. Everything can be spiritualized, but the base remains the body."

"I have wondered if it is partly because we have not given attention to this in a spirit-filled way, then it comes back––through the backdoor, so to speak—in less than ideal and fallen ways."

"So it is. Avoidance, turning one's face, does not work toward full actualization. For all that is gifted to you is worthy of full reflection and meditative focus."

"I am surprised at this image, but I should not be. These 'lesser members' are still members, and we should see what they can teach us. They are at our base, a focus of attraction, and generativity of new life; and they are intensely pleasurable. That said, they can easily be misused and lead to problems in their fallen outlets."

"Yes, you know much and there is more to learn and discover too."

"What's next?" I wondered.

"Receive something simple and be surprised," said the Light Being.

CHAPTER VI
A FLOWER, A GEM

I close my eyes for an image: a flower bright yellow, pendulous yet an opening with frilled petals, glowing light, attracting something?

The Light Being reflects, "The flower is like an archetype of the soul, a simplified architecture of the soul. For everything is what it is, but everything also relates to the essence of things."

"If I am that large and bright of a flower, I have to allow the long-billed bird to lance myself, so that my food may be shared."

"In living we partake in wounding. Such it is that the seemingly simple things teach us things of depth. You have imagined, now let us journey," suggested the Light Being.

The landscape became a series of large, rolling red surfaces, banded with chasms between them, and I realized I was on the petals of a huge flower.

As we walked, the petal gradually dipped to its center, a living fountain of rising ovules. Beautifully sculpted, fleshy and graced with golden grains of pollen. It made me think that sexuality of a type was at the center of more than this flower, but of the universe.

It was living and a living light shone from within. There was not a word or a person there, which my imagination was wont to place, for they are latent there. But the pure form was enough, and it signed a presence deeper within it, not confined or shown by word or by the form of a person.

"Bathe for a moment in that something, and leave it for a moment unnamed and undefined," the Light Being directed.

I am cleft open and light shines from that cleft to the outer confines of my skin. Then a sword enters me and bursts into the concretions that obstruct the flow of this light and love.

"Thank you. I'm sure this is needed."

"Every day, do this," said the Light Being.

Just as I am about to close my eyes, I think *black flower*. Then I close them and imagine a growth that is dark and more undefined, like a fungus but not really living — something heavier that has weight that holds me down. Then a sword appears in my hands and I slash it open. I rear up a crystal shining a bright light, extending its rays, so that my gifted light shines.

"It is interesting how one must slay, to allow life and new life to fully express from oneself. Perhaps it is easy to direct this 'slaying' to others in the hope new life be generated, when it should be oneself."

"To sacrifice is the paradoxical generator of life," the Light Being affirmed. "The temple of Jerusalem was of old, seen as a place of sacrifice. It not only held the Presence, but revealed it as the engine of life. This is the sign of Francis's stigmata, and the mystical seven steps of Bonaventure, in which new life is gained by sacrifice."

"I suppose no one wants to slay that within us which needs to be slain. For we cannot see that as it truly is, and we, in fact, nurture what would hold us back. If I can at least in prayer do what is necessary, and maybe it will open the way for action to occur. For by myself I cannot do what is necessary, but maybe if I become more filled with grace, the action needed will occur."

"Yes, immerse yourself," said the Light Being, "and expression and action will flow, for it will be its nature to do so."

A plethora of images/messages already in a lived day, and yet it is morning.

The Light Being was not finished. "Give yourself to me, for I have given myself to you. The heart and eyes of the Presence in the temple;

the capacity for decision so that you don't sacrifice your son to Molech. These are enough.

"You are blessed with having time to feel spiritual impulses and to act on them. It is a blessing and a responsibility."

"There is so much light if one but seeks it," I reflected. "I thank the universe for what it has given and what it will yet give. In a short time relative to the scheme of things, I will have passed this earth."

"Too early yet to think this way. You have much to complete."

"I have not closed my eyes and seen how all this will be brought together."

"So do so."

"We love. We do not discriminate, young and old––all. None are excluded. All bear the heart of God inside."

An image: Thorns. *Love brings its own special pain. The thorns encircle the heart. We are pierced when we love. Let not this piercing keep us from being bold.*

"We love. We go where the spirit leads us...."

"Let us be suffused with light, a loving light coming from the heart encircled by thorns."

"The thorns drip with blood and from the blood comes a sweet aroma. Blood has a distinctive smell, but holy bread even more so."

"We are asked to dig further and further until we find the precious gem we need to receive."

CHAPTER VII
WRESTLING

*T**hanks. Give thanks and accept thanks.* The thought came quickly today. Not an image, but words. We are thanked and we give thanks.

"The universe is thankful for whatever good is done," said the Light Being. "Though seemingly small, many things start that way and then build. With the grace of the Presence, it can build into something no one would have thought possible.

"I hardly believe it possible. Maybe I expect too little. But things have taken years, and there is not yet a breakthrough."

"You have made the 'breakthrough' already, something bigger than published words. A child brought into the world––what is a bigger thing than that! Mirrored in the child of the Presence that was the greatest act of love, the emptying. This act encapsulates, allows for service and for death, a real emptying that shows love."

"I have already been given what I think I am asking for. This project is not complete, and I fear my attention to words and knowing become the focus rather than loving."

"Wrestle, my friend. As long as you wrestle, you are well. The answer is in the wrestling. It is more real than a sudden artificial solution, or an instant attainment."

"It takes time to wrestle, which I have been given. It seems a simple work, but yet it is hard. Is there not a false pleasure to turn away from the work too soon, to leave it unfinished, while I browse elsewhere, and things do not add up and are not shared?

"I fear I am just doing for myself, if I leave it there. I pray for the grace of completion, which I sorely need.

"I don't think we fully overcome our limitations, but we do press against them and grace does marvels. But do we really overcome them?"

"Perhaps we learn to wrestle with them better. It is time to close your eyes and draw inward again, for much lies below, even if you only go a little beneath the surface."

I wrestle with a variety of thoughts and impressions and nothing distills.

"Try again."

Smooth, flow—the way. They are words, and sayings follow, 'Make straight the way. The Dao as the Way.'

"Do not fight yourself. If you wrestle, wrestle with the other. It is more interesting that way."

Me "Why is it so difficult for me? I imagine the smooth and the flowing as water by the gulf. But I know there is also an area called the *washing machine that* would just as well drown me. For every image there is a counter-image. For now, I seek that calmer spot within myself. Yet there is so much wrestling to get there!"

Imagine floating in a substance, a soul substance filled with a subtle glowing light that seeps up, takes in all the tension of my body, or rather, all the bad tension. Leave only the tension that will allow me to move forward and accomplish what I need. Call this *Forward Floating.*

"Yes, move toward the area of greater light. In this light, use its strength to touch aspects of yourself and those who are in the dark and those who are suffering. In the light we can endure our own and other's crosses."

"In looking this over, I think of the greener light. Green is new growth, the green promises life. The green is young."

"Yes, you are to look into the mirror and see yourself younger. Though having that, stay clear of sins, even small ones."

"Youth is a matter of purity, it seems ... as archaic as that word is, as little talked about as it is. "

"The green light bathes you and it is healing," adds the Light Being. "But it does not stop death. For there is a switch when things give out, and you go fully over to the Presence, who would have you shed this constant of your world, so that only love is left behind and new 'clothes' are outfitted for you."

"I have emptied out so much space, so hopefully there is some for the Presence to be with me and give me the light to do what little I can do."

"Even as I get older, I seem to look out at grownups. And when the crowd is in their twenties, it is more like an equivalent. Perhaps I have remained too totipotential to finish things, to carry them to the end."

"So when you say, 'It is finished,' you have born the pain and what awaits is new life."

"As you get older, you get closer to that point. Should we fear it? Should not time expand allowing us to reach that point?"

"Close your eyes."

A moment before and the thought is, *Act and do not fear*. It is better to act than to hold back in fear.

"There is a sense of space opening, of something to be filled. That things can become organized and progress made. Then I draw back to reality that I am viewing a totipotentiality not yet actualized into a charged path."

"So, you have reached the zero point where directions lay open and the path is not yet decided."

"To act and to move. Sometimes I like to stay out of sight and be myself, for myself, in my own wondrous thoughts."

"But there is no sense of completion, the excitement of touching others. Just a simple conversation...."

"You are wrestling again. It is good to wrestle," complimented the Light Being. "Wrestle in the light.

"Then the deeper light says: I will open the way for you. I will show things to you. You will not be left with a blank. In some ways you will return to what was before, but the time has drastically changed."

"So all I can do is to remain with an open heart and hope that the courage is added somehow. That the general prayer be made and that the blanks be filled as time emerges."

"*I am with you. You are not alone.* So we have company along the way, even when we think we are by ourselves."

"We need to learn to be with others. I can't be halfway there and thinking of a break or doing something else. I have to be fully present, not wanting to be elsewhere. Give me the grace to do that!"

'*Keep going forward,*' the words before I close my eyes. I feel like I am coming closer to the track.

"Close your eyes again and see what lies deeper, what message emerges after a passage of time."

"There is too much noise and dissonance in my environment."

"Try again."

A song plays with mystical melody. *You can't get what you want.* The words are slow, each sentence a struggle.

"Words, sentences keep us alive. Then something more than that—words enfleshed, bringing a body to you."

"Dig deeper. Love, find the love at night. The closer needs to be strong to win the game. We can't go down in defeat each day."

"What is closer?" I ask.

"How about an attempt at prayer, a prayer with the family? Ask God's grace to close the night, for it is like dying, giving up on the day. End well."

"Maybe at night, a prophet reading is in order. Jeremiah is arriving."

"Keep wrestling is the only rule, the absolute in a sense. Then let love be born, for you don't want to wrestle too long, lest you tire and give up.

"Let nothing be there for a space and do not try to fill it. Leave the space for something to come.

"We love you. We are never far away. That is sufficient for today."

CHAPTER VIII
POWER

What's next? *Power.* Things are done. The Presence is one who acts and does, though it may be hidden, though it may wait to be asked, though it may be so blatant as to be missed.

"Why do I look back and see but a gaping space––like what have I done—and how old I am now?"

"You have birthed a son, the largest project anyone can do. You have put forward voices that were unheard in *Cry of the Invisible.* You have worked as a teacher with children. Now you are rich in time—a gift to you."

"I have never looked back at my life and wondered how I could have been great or famous, compared to what is manifest now. But I did my work and moved on. I did not always complete, or finish the action, to say 'it is finished.'"

"The biggest goal and biggest gift is to draw close to the Presence of all, and to draw others that way. So much of your writing is that, and one day it will be more available to all. Light cannot be hidden."

I know not where to start, but to close my eyes and see what is given. *Be with me.* Simple enough. Three words.

"But when I turn to the night, I sometimes do not close well."

"Keep my presence close at all times, make stabs through it, and then the opening of my presence will become stronger and find the answer that refreshes you.

"Perhaps my sanctity is attaching itself to you despite your failings and unawareness, though it's funny how a simple mirror can give you a clue."

"It seems that my voice and yours merge at times, that we complete each other sentences…"

"And so it is. Our goal is to release you from any bondage, so the spirit flows, and then what happens, happens."

"I look at myself and it seems failure, all those years dealing with bureaucracy at Social Services."

"You put yourself in harm's way and some good 'harm' was done."

"Now I have time. I come home to a year-old dog and a six-year-old child about to become seven."

"Be with me. Then how can you go wrong? Present the self in all its good and all its faults. What more can you do? You are where you are at this moment. Call the prayer one of presentation—an honest presentation."

"Hello Light Being. I have a loss over an object that was expensive and does not work now, though there is some hope of resuscitating it, but it is probably necessary to discard this huge item, which is hard enough, and then maybe get a lesser one that works better."

"Let me wash over you with some light. Let his fire of trial help purify you, be an opportunity for purifying. Let go of any result with the object. It may or may not resolve, but you know you have resources to ultimately handle this issue."

"Let me wash more in your being, your light and love. I want to be present fully to my son."

"We love you and we are putting you on a healing track."

"My son! I don't want to deliver him to the empire track!"

"We will guide you!"

"I thank you for coming near when I hurt, even it is a small issue. I am sorry for my materialism that takes that loss harder than a human one. How far have I gone to feel that? To feel more deeply the loss of an object over a person?"

"Use the pain for purgative purposes that you may come closer to the Presence and others. Look for good in all things!"

"Still, I hurt, and I don't know how to move forward. This small thing wells up like an obsession."

"You are stronger than that. You are gifted, and like Jeremiah, I will protect you."

"I realize this pain is also a testing of sorts, and that this testing turns things for good."

"Clearly seeing the loss and harm, then moving on to the next step that resolves things even better. That's the promise we give. Despite pain and suffering at the end awaits a glory. We are here for you."

"I'm sorry. I feel the weight of it all. So many with crisis and mine the far lesser. On top of it, I'm so tired I should sleep instead I fall into thoughts of lust."

"Return always and become stronger. Resolve of ways to do battle. Sharpen your swords, and be there, still for others. It's love that saves us all in the end."

"Thank you for the words of encouragement. It is time to close my eyes."

"Between desire and lust, dip into the pool of pain. Approach and wrestle with what presents itself, whether sin or grace."

"In your desire you seek beauty. You seek virtues. There are better ways. What are they? How can you tend to things and stay within boundaries, the welcome embrace?"

"Let me turn to something else instead. Let it be you. Let me stop things and offer myself, and just lie down and absorb, take in the grace."

"Sounds good. Even to do that when you feel pain is a good idea. Let the love wash over you. Accepting always. To receive is as important as giving in the cosmic scheme of things."

Anger arises. Anger leads to mood, leads to action. God, how do you deal with the anger?

Your action in history is a communication, and the ones who receive it wonder and maybe figure it out, or not.

"As you say, the anger leads to action. So anger can be a good thing. It must be contained by love."

"Give me the strength to endure the time before. Anger wants action now. The unsettling I experience now is a change of status, a movement of being. That is an exciting thing; it also holds some peril."

"Peril simply means that you lean on us more, that you seek your strength from the Source."

CHAPTER IX
TESTING

I blow out a breath of stress as I find my brother diminished by illness and treatment.

"Do not worry. Take the moment."

"Let me pause and be bathed in the light. Why are we so weak?"

"Crisis exposes hidden faults. It releases hidden tension. It was already there, merely seeking an outlet. The energy must be released."

"I have time, for good or worse, to experience the daily and not so daily shocks of life. I am not distracted by the demands of the normal work world.

"I read the history of ages, but it is filled with inhumanity and the death of those who help the poor. Of course, the power seekers die just as much or even more frequently."

"Rest in me. Enough will be given. Handle what is close, and handle what is far, though it is close in another way."

"I am wounded by my sin. My failures of inaction are before me. My missing years––what could have been—haunt me. Yet I am very much alive and have much promise, though the word promise is typically reserved for youth."

"It is not how much, but how deep, how much you present— stand before."

"I cannot but do so much, for I become exhausted, emptied...."

"Let me fill you. Stay still."

"Let my body fill with your light. Let me close my eyes and let this happen. From my feet to the crown of my head.

"I don't have the words in me. The flow has stopped. In its place a stress.

"But I have time to face the stresses and to ameliorate them, to give them form and then kill them. But in-between I feel them more fully.

"The day's given anxieties crowd me. Perhaps I have too much time and give them space. But they are my inner life.

"It is a weight, a block, a heaviness. Maybe no more needs to be said, rather something done."

"Let go of the weight, drop the block, release the heaviness. We are light and lightness and always near you.

"Take a deep breath and release the tension into the air, where it is absorbed by the heavenly healers."

The message comes over an electronic text almost a thousand miles away. Emotions causing illness, the feeling of not being wanted. It comes down to love in the end.

"I find it so hard to visit because I don't want to go into the pain. Who wants the cross? Yet we have to ask for the strength to go into it."

"Again, bathe in the light. We take our natural baths, but we need a spiritual bath every so often as well! Try it! Clean all of your body.

"The bath comes from outside, atop you, but also imagine it coming from within you, from your center."

"What do I do?"

"Love, that is all you can do. Respond. Come to your brother only if he wants you to come."

"He sets barriers, saying no, then needing yes. But I think things can be engineered." "Go into the fire. Sometimes there is not much else choice. To serve is to be baptized, to drink the cup of dying to self, of being taken away from one's comfort zone."

"I am wrestling against it. Yet I know I will go. Part of the uncertainty is knowing when to go and having permission to go."

"There is too much to do: old friends, old missions."

"It is like dying, but it is also a new life. It is funny how the challenges don't diminish."

"In this dying one goes into their core."

"I am deep in my pain. I sometimes lose the night. Shouldn't that time of dying/going to sleep be a time of ascent, of joining, not of straying?"

"In that pain, search for the Presence. Remember, in denial there is a pleasure, perhaps the higher pleasure."

"My words become fewer as I go toward the center."

"Go toward the center. It is not the number of words, but the unworded feeling."

"Where do I go from here? It seems so hard to do."

"Add incrementally, things add up."

"Nothing. There needs to be nothing initially. It is not a cleared path for something good to fill, for the Presence to come. If I am filled, how will something potentially greater come?"

"In the morning bathe and shave. Bathe in the light, shave off the excess, the distraction. Your life is your life, and the sacred is all around. There is sacredness in speech; there is sacredness in silence. There is sacredness in being with others. There is sacredness in being apart."

"I have more time, but necessity reigns as to the parameters."

"Touch me. The words are surprising, for isn't it the Presence that touches us? Does the Source, the Presence, have a body that can be touched?"

"If I who have made beings who can touch ... am I not the source of all touch? I touch lips that then flow out my words."

"Conquer. Conquer zones of godlessness. Conquer zones of self that are not spirituality or productive in an effusive way."

"Write, not just for yourself."

"There will come a time when I write for the world more. I focus and ask for the grace that comes to be as it is given to me. I am unworthy to approach, to even speak. I feel my purity disappear, and that I will be abandoned."

"We don't abandon, but we call to perfection. The energy you save can be directed outwards (and inwards) into discovery shared with the world.

"We want to share our being and wealth with those who open up, to those who cry out. Paradoxically, those who fail may open up more in their wound."

"My wound, my emotion... Let me feel what I must feel. Let me do what I must do."

⸺⬤⸺

SO WE GO FORWARD AND, by doing what is necessary, achieve a type of inner peace.

The irony that taking on the cross leads us to relax in the deepest sense. For the Presence grants rest to those who do what is right.

"So let us rest, for all the time we cannot be working and worrying about the morrow."

"Yes, I feel mortality knocking, not a strong knock but knocking nonetheless, and the time we have is limited. Then we let go."

"Even if you do no more, you have done much in love. So add on and do some more, if first for your son, then spouse, then family. We are here only so long."

"Yes, it is closing toward the final chapters. We have lived and done so much amazing stuff, but then it seems, we have equally failed––and which is more amazing, despairing?"

"Don't worry. We are with you and even stronger, as time goes forward. Yet, the temptations to slow you and to hold things back are not absent."

"Give me the strength to keep my focus on, to finish strong in the day. To finish strong may be the willingness to let go, so the early morning can be a creative time."

Do not fear your lacks, a message after closing my eyes.

"The weaknesses are opportunities for grace because you see them as something lacking, you know, to work at them."

"I am weak. I am feeling empty of something overflowing."

"Join that emptiness. Do not fear it, or dispense with it. For that is but an opening."

"I feel a social lack. I need to make a plan during the week. A lot of things flow through that opening. The need for a device to reach beyond. The need for meetings during the day.

I close my eyes and see what happens.

"I am close and far. You need but invite me. And speak to me. Do I not answer?"

"You do in your gentle way. Yet it pierces me, as it's true. The love is so true underlying whatever is said. And tears come so readily."

"Open a channel. Service is good because it sets aside the self, so there is room for me. I am humble and do not come without invitation—though sometimes I am part of the whirlwind of life and enter, seemingly unasked. For I know the deepest desire and often give what is not yet known, but yet is the deeper desire."

The message on the medal of St. Clare: the poorest person has the infinite God within, a treasure. So what more do we need? What loss compares to that? What perspective else do we need?

"Yes, rest in the infinite, but you are to go out into the world. For there is both the vertical and horizontal, and one does both."

Amen.

ABOUT JOHN

It is so sad, my brother failing and having the light. But if we are drawn to God, then the real life awaits ahead! John was so certain and celebratory about this deep hope buried within all of us, and to which he spoke explicitly. We need the hope of eternal life to set things in context, to reduce our anxieties. To stop the wars, to have peace. It is the answer, if ever there was one. But it is not one that comes easily. It is seen from the cross. It was seen after caring for his mom and dad for seven years.

So maybe I will write "Dear John letters" for the conversation can continue. It is all finite. We are all running toward the finish line, running out of earth time and heading into eternal time with no measured time at all.

We must hold on some, and let go a lot, if we are to live freely.

God is so tender and gracious. Opting to be with John so he could share before taking him home....

John thought he had a thousand or more essays in him. Yet what is written, is written, and that is a lot.

Oh, the hurt and the peace!

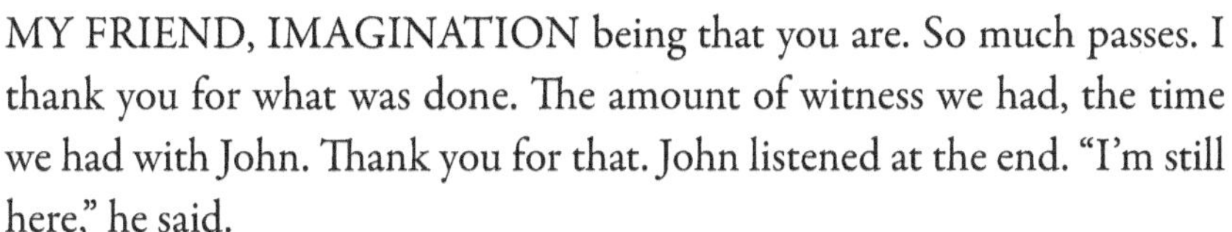

MY FRIEND, IMAGINATION being that you are. So much passes. I thank you for what was done. The amount of witness we had, the time we had with John. Thank you for that. John listened at the end. "I'm still here," he said.

I don't know if this awakens pain more or not, but I need to close my eyes again, and I feel on the edge, there is peace.

"Peace, my son. Great joy awaits you in heaven. Nothing will keep you from the love of God."

"I don't know what to say. Deep down I feel undeserving, that I have failed too much. Yet, you assure me that it is not so, that the door is not locked. The feeling of heaven assured is a deep peace. Yet I know one doesn't rest with that, but one pursues one's passion, one's journey to the kingdom right now."

"You are right. We are with you. Things worked out well enough. There is not perfection until heaven. We love you. Keep pure. Keep with it. You have some of John with you on your journey."

Again, I am here, presenting myself. My letter this morning is broken. I feel, however, a clarity of spirit come upon me. Why have I traded it away for so little at times? So I close myself and ask for a word.

"We love you. It is that simple, and then out of that love comes more love. We love no matter what. Let us change, even deeper, to a degree more. You can look back and see there is a lot of love already. But there is more…"

"John said he wasn't a writer, but he became one, with the grace of God. He had a wonderful ability that I sensed even before. John had a surprising genre present within him.

"I feel there is not enough time. I feel I will get sidetracked once again, but maybe not. Maybe with the death of John and writing to him, I can keep on track. I pray that it be so."

"We will help you finish well!"

AFTERWARD

A few months before my brother passed, I imagined taking a contemplative journey with a spiritual being. The purpose of the work evolved, and it came to focus on finding ways to release my work and creativity into the world. Other than a book of first-person oral histories from homeless or psychiatrically diagnosed persons, and a handful of professional articles, I possessed a lot of work that was unpublished. A literary agent for over five years has been trying, but nothing had succeeded. Then a chance sequence of events occurred: an offer by a hybrid publisher to publish my work, finding out that I would have to pay them; then a neighbor across the street giving me the lead to *Draft2Digital*. This became the door that has made my body of work available.

But it was only after my brother passed that I had the impetus to write a blog of letters for others, to break open my shell to share with others. From there, work written over the course of a lifetime is being released, as well as other person's work. How doors open, how providence provides a way is remarkable.

The work being published, I believe, has enduring messages that will cross generational spans. I have not taken the standard writing classes, nor had a professional editor from a publishing house to help me with this cause. Yet, having read a considerable portion of the world literature, and the sheer persistence of years, along with valuable suggestions from friends, has led me to become a writer.

This work is largely autobiographical, in that it details the spiritual struggle involved in sharing our gifts with the world. For writers early on, and I include myself, tend to guard their work and not so readily share. But the good is expansive, and the call to share is there. This is one writer's struggle, who gains help from an Imaginary Being.

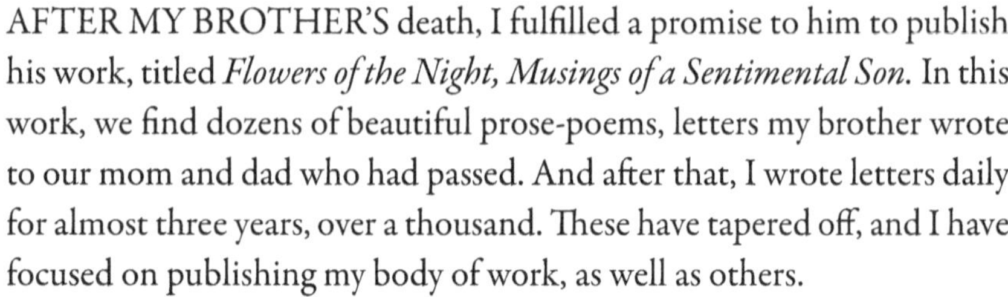

AFTER MY BROTHER'S death, I fulfilled a promise to him to publish his work, titled *Flowers of the Night, Musings of a Sentimental Son.* In this work, we find dozens of beautiful prose-poems, letters my brother wrote to our mom and dad who had passed. And after that, I wrote letters daily for almost three years, over a thousand. These have tapered off, and I have focused on publishing my body of work, as well as others.

The irony and blessing is how events of five years ago are being fulfilled, and that once what is imagined, comes to be.

Don't miss out!

Visit the website below and you can sign up to receive emails whenever Michael A. Susko publishes a new book. There's no charge and no obligation.

https://books2read.com/r/B-A-GJLJ-BIOSB

BOOKS 2 READ

Connecting independent readers to independent writers.

Did you love *The Imagination Being*? Then you should read *Flowers of the Night: Musings from a Sentimental Son*[1] by John E. Susko!

[2]

The author would awake in the early morning hours, dictating prose-poems that he addresses to his mother and father who have passed. These extraordinary letters explore topics which embrace paradoxes: how seasons transform into eternity, how silence is filled with sound, and how our neighbors are our gold. Our writer, who has been diagnosed with cancer, comes upon a newfound gift to express his soul. We invite you to take a journey with John who desires to be your friend and share his uncommon vision of beauty and truth with you.

Read more at https://www.allroneofus.com/.

---

1. https://books2read.com/u/mgGpwx

2. https://books2read.com/u/mgGpwx

Also by Michael A. Susko

A Couple Through Time
Down Below and the Archon's Castle
Up Above and the Runaway
Across the Gulf and Journey Into Un-Time
On the Bay and a Child Found
In the Wild and Do One Wild Thing
On the Mountain and Two Are Missing
To the Beginning and Journey Through Here

Archetypal Worlds
Alwon in Another World: An Archetypal Voyage
Line On the Wall
The Alien's Gift
The Gold People
Spider Woman and the Timeroc
Quill Ears & the Other Earth
Darkwood and Dual with the Shadow Side
Giant Under the Mountain

Early Humanity

The Firekeeper
Child of the Elements

Haikus and Photos
Flowers and Haikus
Haikus and Photos: Guatemalan Highlands
Haikus and Photos: Water Birds and Reflections
Haikus and Photos: Seasons of New River
Haikus and Photos: Yosemite Wilderness
Haikus and Photos: California Coast
Haikus and Photos: Canadian Rockies
Haikus and Photos: Hawaii's Exotic Landscapes
Haikus and Photos: Vienna, People with Buildings and Art
Haikus and Photos: Slovakian Castles and Hamlets
Haikus and Photos: Berlin, Light and Dark
Haikus and Photos: New Orleans, City of Immigrants
Haikus and Photos: Antietam Wind and Spirits
Haikus & Photos: Plant Abstractions
Haikus and Photos: Appalachian Beauty
Haikus and Photos: Urban Farm in Sandtown
Haikus and Photos: New York Heights and Ground

Little Lion
The Lion and the Chameleon
The Elephant and the Chameleons

Nature Haikus & Photos
Haikus and Photos: Butterflies and Flowers

Haikus and Photos: Presence at Penn Bluff
Haikus & Photos: Mystery Form at Penn Bluff
Haikus and Photos: Essences at Penn Bluff
Haikus and Photos: World Archetypes at Penn Bluff

The Dreaming Series
Sleek Back
Streak and Cave Bear Dreaming
Moby and Marsupial Mole Dreaming

The Dream World Trilogy
Delphi, the Time Thief, and the Dream World
Detinna and the Cave God
The Resistance & the Empire

Transformational Stories
Caseness and Narrative: Contrasting Approaches to People
Psychiatrically Labelled
Transformative Experiences, Psychiatric Research, and Informed
Consent
Transformational Stories: Voices for True Healing in Mental Health

Writings from Street People
Street Images
Street Images II

Standalone
The Little People & the Time-Rider
Animal Spell: A Gospel Story With a Transformational Twist
Ten Pulses of Evolution & the Surprising Nature of Evolutionary Time
Up Above and Down Below
Life's Dynamic Vulnerability: A Paradigm Shift in Biology
Alien Ally
The Generation of LIfe: Imagery, Ritual and Experiences in Deep Caves
Twelve Suspects
2084: Clash of the Cults
Bats in the Future
Guard of the Dead and Other Gospel Stories
The Imagination Being
Ten Traits of Empire that Every Person Should Know
Aging and Renewal: Living the Full Life
The Meaning, Beauty & Mystery of Dreams: Seven Guidelines and
Seven Tools for Listening
A Rosetta Key for History: The Generational Pattern of Time

Watch for more at https://www.allroneofus.com/.

About the Author

As a young man, the author had experiences of a symbolic world, which helped him to envision fictional ones that are archetypically sound. He also draws upon his teaching of college classes on the symbolism of indigenous cultures and paleolithic art found in deep caves. Last, his familiarity with his own dreams, and teaching classes on dream interpretation has helped to keep him in touch with the symbolic world.

Read more at https://www.allroneofus.com/.

About the Publisher

AllrOneofUs Publishing seeks out work which will make a novel and qualitative addition to the world literature, and one that will last across generations. Many of these persons are in the later part of their life and have made exemplary contributions which are unrecognized. To cite a few examples, we recommend Rich Mullin's *Ethics and the Full-breasted Richness of Life*, John Susko's *Flowers of the Night: Musings from a Sentimental Son,* and Dr. Curtis Adams' *Psychosis and the Humpty Dumpty Story.*